OM
Life's Gentle Reminders

Kamini Wood

Published by
WSA Publishing
301 E 57th Street, 4th fl
New York, NY 10022

Copyright © 2020 by Kamini Wood

All rights reserved. No part of this book may be reproduced or transmitted in any form or by in any means, electronic or mechanical, including photocopying, recording, or by any information storage and retrieval system, without the written permission of the Publisher, except where permitted by law.

Manufactured in the United States of America, or in the United Kingdom when distributed elsewhere.

Wood, Kamini
    OM: Life's Gentle Reminders
    LCCN: 2020900560
    ISBN: 978-1-951943-01-1
    eBook: 978-1-951943-02-8

Cover design by: Natasha Clawson
Copyediting and interior design by: Claudia Volkman
Cover Photo by: Teresa Porter

www.itsauthenticme.com

DEDICATION

For my family, who inspire me daily

TABLE OF CONTENTS

Introduction vii
Get Messy 1
Friendships 3
AI . . . Friend or Foe? 5
What My Morning Traffic Jam Taught Me 7
Listen to the Flashing Yellow 9
Your Choices Are Yours—Honor Them 11
Grinding and Gritting 13
Boiling Water Isn't Always Bad 15
Foundations 17
Looking Sideway May Be the Answer 21
Acknowledging the Cracks 23
Making the Turn 25
Strip It Down 27
How Do You Know When It's Time to Leap? 29
Directionally Challenged 31
To Be Stuck or Unstuck 33
To Know or Not to Know? 35
How Tight Is Your Grip? 37
Out of Routine 39
If You Can't Duct Tape It 41
Judge Judy 43
It's Just Hair 45
Toy Story 4 47
To Each Shell Her Own 51
Over the Rainbow 53
But That's Not What the Recipe Says 55
Unexpected Growth 57
Boundary Bubble 59
Does the Shoe Fit? 61
Blisters Get You Ready 63

Building Blocks	65
It Was Always Burning	67
Walking on Eggshells	69
The Blind Spot	71
The Moth versus the Butterfly	73
Lost in the Maze	75
Authentic . . . One of Today's Buzzwords	77
Piv . . .oooot!	79
It May Not Be Shorter	81
I Never Noticed That Before . . .	83
Hot Coffee	85
Dense Fog Advisory	87
The Balloon	89
I Have Bermuda Grass	91
Where's My Charger?	93
Haunted Houses	95
I Can See Clearly Now	97
The Dirt Is Sometimes More Than Just Dirt	99
How Thin Is the Butter?	101
I See the Top	103
Behind the Scenes	105
What Does the End Say?	107
Backdraft	109
Bunched-Up Socks	111
Zippers	113
The New Owner	115
I'm Sorry	117
The DMV	119
Squeezed In Like Sardines	121
A Bottleneck	123
Lessons from an Old Dog	125
The Lost Keys	127

INTRODUCTION

I AM A first-generation American. As I grew up, I tried to fit in so that I didn't stand out too much, and I did that by working hard, getting good grades, people-pleasing, putting others before myself, and always wanting to help solve other people's problems.

I carried all this weight into adulthood. It was motherhood that made me see it. I realized that my kids were showing signs of becoming people-pleasing perfectionists and writing a similar story to mine.

I sought support. I consulted with a therapist, and I also hired a coach to give me the tools I needed to find myself again.

I recognized that I didn't have my own identity because I was so busy fixing other people's issues. More importantly, I realized that I had told myself I was responsible for their happiness.

I began to set boundaries and pay attention to my own needs and wants.

And I will be completely transparent: As I started to shift my focus on ME, there were some who were uncomfortable because they were used to old Kamini. But I finally had a new sense of self and purpose. And I also realized that those who truly loved me just needed time to adjust. They will still love me, because I am still me—I am just a more confident me.

I felt realigned with my self-worth, and I was able to be more authentic with my relationships.

Now I'm living a life that's 100 percent authentic and true to who I really am. I no longer try and people-please, I'm no longer a hostage to other people's expectations, and I'm free of worrying about what others think of me.

After going through my own struggles and breakthroughs, I wanted to channel my experience and help other women going through the same struggles. Because if they don't break the pattern, they will endure a lifelong internal battle, one that will be passed on for generations to come if not addressed and solved.

I have compiled this book of short analogies to offer a new way of looking at things. I find that when we can relate our everyday experiences to the greater experience of building ourselves into the self-leaders we are meant to be, we are able to make smaller mindset shifts that allow us to see things differently and make a bigger difference.

GET MESSY

Your sacred space is where you can find yourself again and again.
JOSEPH CAMPBELL

I SEEM TO be late to new trends. So only recently did I watch an episode from Marie Kondo.

In case you have not seen her, she goes into people's homes and helps them declutter. The first step in the process is to take everything in a room and pile it up in the center of the room. She then goes through a process of asking if an item brings the owner joy. If not, she instructs her clients to thank the items prior to getting rid of them.

Honestly, as I was watching this, I was a little disturbed. The people on the show had A LOT of stuff. And it all seemed a little "woo-woo" to me.

But then I started to think... this idea of pulling things out of my "closet," evaluating what I "needed" or could "use," and throwing out the rest is actually something I had done in the past in my personal life.

As a new mom, I had the feeling that I had no control over anything. It felt like I couldn't meet my child's needs. I couldn't meet my spouse's needs. There was an overwhelming feeling of overwhelm.

Finally, by admitting it out loud—all the emotions, feelings, stressors, worries, everything going through my mind—I was finally able to gain the mental space to evaluate where things were, what thoughts served me, and how to move forward on this new journey of being a mom.

In essence, I had to pull out of the "closet" (aka my mind) everything I was thinking and feeling.

It was messy.

But once it was all out there, there was space. Space to figure out the next step forward.

If you could, just for today, allow all your feelings—good, bad, pretty, ugly—rise to the surface, without judgment, how would you show up differently?

FRIENDSHIPS

*If you change the way you look at things,
the things you look at change.*
WAYNE DYER

LET'S FACE IT: relationships in general are hard. You trust someone. You are close to them. And then something changes.

You grow. They grow in a different way. You change. They change—or they lack change. And it turns out that what you were getting from that relationship no longer serves you.

But there is still such a huge part of you that feels bad or feels like you should make it work.

Should is the key word here.

One of my clients was really struggling because one of her best friends had chosen to go down a path she did not agree with. Her friend was suddenly interested in drugs and alcohol, something my client avoided.

The struggle was real, though. The desire to hold on to the past relationship. The desire to keep things as they were. But what we talked through and worked through was that, as time evolves, sometimes friendships reach a point where they no longer serve you. They are not helping you grow or, more importantly, are not supporting your growth.

When we do things because we should, we are hostage

to expectations rather than being a self-leader. Rather than being true to ourselves.

It is hard. I will not deny that. When you have been friends with someone or been in a relationship with someone for a while, it is like a death.

Here are some tips to help with the change:

- Give yourself time and space to mourn the relationship.
- Give yourself time and space to figure out if there is a level of friendship you can maintain. Is it that instead of being BFFs, now this person can be more of a cordial acquaintance? Or maybe simply it's best for the person to be someone you simply say hi and bye to.
- Honor what you shared with this person in the past.
- Start looking forward to beginning new relationships.
- Look forward to possibility.

What if you allowed yourself to step back from relationships that are no longer serving you? How would you show up differently in the relationships that are working and are healthy? Would you be more present in them?

AI . . . FRIEND OR FOE?

> *We delight in the beauty of the butterfly but rarely admit the changes it has gone through to achieve that beauty.*
>
> MAYA ANGELOU

I WALKED INTO Panera today to order a sandwich and sit and work. I don't know if you have ever been to a Panera Bread, but they have self-serve kiosks where you can place your order. Or if you prefer, you can still order with a human.

The kiosk area was completely free. No one around them. The line to order with the cashier was ten people deep.

I started to wonder why people would choose to stand and wait in line to place their order instead of simply navigating their online kiosk?

Was it because people did not know how to work the kiosk app?

Could it be the fear of messing up their order that made them choose to wait in a twenty-minute line to place an order rather than walk up to a computer-based system?

How often do we simply lose time because we are too afraid to ask for help? Or too afraid to that we won't get something "right" that we avoid trying it in the first place?

WHAT MY MORNING TRAFFIC JAM TAUGHT ME

Nothing has any power over me other than that which I give it through my conscious thoughts.
TONY ROBBINS

THIS MORNING AS my daughter and I headed southbound on the highway, I noticed flashing lights in the distance heading north. As we approached, we saw a car stopped in the left lane. A police car, lights on, had pulled up behind the car. Both cars were completely blocking the left travel lane.

As we continued in our direction, I kept peering to the left and took notice of the line of cars that was forming. And forming. And forming.

My daughter commented, "Look at those cars. They are stuck. They just can't move anywhere."

This reminded me of what happens when I get down on myself about something. For instance, when something does not go as planned, what went wrong is the only thing I can focus on. Like when I made a birthday cake for my daughter and it came out lopsided. All I could think about was the lopsidedness of that cake. I could not enjoy the fact that my daughter was pleased that I had made the cake on my own for her. All I could think was that it wasn't perfect. I had failed. No other thoughts were able to come forward because they were completely stuck behind the negative ones.

Negative thoughts can paralyze us, much like those cars being stopped in the travel lane paralyzed any other vehicles from moving forward.

So, the next time a negative thought comes up, what if you simply acknowledged it, and then kindly moved it "off to the side of the road"? What if you let its "engine" cool, knowing you could deal with it later?

Would you be able to move forward with your day more effectively?

LISTEN TO THE FLASHING YELLOW

*It does not matter how slowly you go
as long as you do not stop.*

CONFUCIUS

EACH AFTERNOON ON my commute, I pass by an elementary school. As I approach the school zone, I see a pair of yellow lights. When these lights are flashing, drivers are reminded that the school zone speed limit is active. That means the speed limit drops from 35 mph to 25 mph.

And each afternoon, as drivers approach these flashing lights, myself included, brake lights begin to shine and cars slow down.

Flashing light = slow down. Simple. We do it.

We do it with our cars, yet we don't do it so easily with our thoughts. Even more, sometimes when we have a negative thought, we really let it run wild. We allow it to run through our minds fast and furious.

What if, just for now, you were able to find a way to remind yourself to breathe? Slow down. Allow your thoughts and emotions to settle. What if you could be 5 percent more aware when your thoughts start running wild and were able to envision a blinking yellow light to remind you to slow down? How would you show up differently?

YOUR CHOICES ARE YOURS— HONOR THEM

You and I are essentially infinite choice-makers. In every moment of our existence, we are in that field of all possibilities where we have access to an infinity of choices.

DEEPAK CHOPRA

A FUNNY THING occurred recently. Something had happened with one of my children, and I attempted to voice my concern. It was evident in the tone of the person I spoke with that my interpretation of the seriousness did not match this other's person's opinion.

A few years ago, when I was stuck as a hostage to expectations, I would have felt bad for even bringing up my concern and would have felt that I was expected to stay quiet and not make waves because it was "disruptive."

What I have learned, though, is that living up to others' expectations or living up to "shoulds" does not work long-term.

We each have our own thoughts, and the reality we live is based on those thoughts. And each thought can be true.

So now, instead of changing my opinion to meet the expectation of "keeping the peace," I quietly and thoughtfully made a decision to remove my child from the situation.

After I made this move, this person I had originally tried to reach out suddenly asked if we could meet.

But here's the thing. I had tried the first time. I had reached out and voiced my concern. When this person did not want to take the time to hear me, that was her choice.

What I did next was simply ask myself, "Was it true that she should have listened to me?" Honestly, the answer was no. It was really none of my business whether or not she chose to hear me. What was true and was my business was what I chose to do with my child.

I made the choice to move on.

If you knew that whatever choices you make were yours and no one else's business, how would your outlook change?

GRINDING AND GRITTING

*I can be changed by what happens to me.
But I refuse to be reduced by it.*

MAYA ANGELOU

I KNOW. GRINDING one's teeth is usually a sign of stress. But that's a topic for a different day.

After several impressions, my mouth guard was ready for pickup. I originally went to the dentist's office thinking it would take only a couple minutes. But instead, picking up the mouth guard was a process.

Why?

The dentist doesn't just hand you the mouth guard. The dental assistant places it in your mouth and tests the bite several times. After each test, she shaved away parts of the guard. This back-and-forth took about half an hour. Finally she polished it.

Before I left, I had to make a follow-up appointment for two weeks out. The receptionist explained that this was totally normal because as I began using the guard, I might feel that some areas were not working or were pinching, and some minor adjustments could be needed. And sometimes everything would be fine and the appointment would be super quick. She also informed me that every six months when I came in for my cleaning, I should bring back the guard so it could be sanitized in order to maintain it.

While I was not expecting such a process with the mouth guard, it certainly got me thinking.

This is really what it's like when we choose to do self-work.

We start with an observation of where we are currently.

We decide to work on certain things.

Some things work, and we keep doing them.

Some things don't serve us, and we make changes.

The process of self-work and moving from expectation hostage to resilient self-leader is a process of symbolic "shaving," learning to change and polish mindsets, thought patterns, behavior patterns, and so on.

And it doesn't end there. We have to be committed to check in with ourselves. We maintain the work. It's not a quick fix, where we can change one thing and move on forever. Just like the mouth guard. It wasn't a quick impression, mold it, and go. It was a process. It required a little bit of patience and work.

But it is so worth it in the end.

If there was one mindset shift you have been thinking about making, what would it be? What would be possible for you?

BOILING WATER ISN'T ALWAYS BAD

*Patience is power. Patience is not an absence of action;
rather it is "timing" it waits on the right time to act,
for the right principles and in the right way.*

Fulton J. Sheen

HAVE YOU EVER made a cup of tea and either the water wasn't hot enough or you didn't let the tea bag steep long enough?

This happened the other day. I made myself a cup of tea, but being in a rush, I did not let the tea bag steep in the hot water long enough. I left the tea bag in for a minute, pulled it out, and ran out the door, mug in hand.

I took a sip of the tea, and it just tasted awful. Vaguely flavored hot water—so weak and ineffective.

It got me thinking about how sitting in "hot water" sometimes is a good thing.

Take emotions. There are times, when they are so heavy or they scare us that all we want to do is avoid them or get out of them as quickly as possible. Because they are like boiling water.

When my daughter was hospitalized for pneumonia, I refused to acknowledge the emotions I was feeling. I was scared. Actually terrified.

She was this tiny thing, so sick, with a fever that would not break. She couldn't keep any food down, and the medicines didn't appear to be helping.

At the time, I just kept going. Going on. Brave face. "I got this" attitude.

Admittedly, sometimes you need to do that. In the moment, in front of my child, I had to do that for her.

But when I was alone, I could have given myself the time to feel. But I didn't. And that ended up causing utter exhaustion.

As a mother, there are definitely times where you have to put on a brave face for your child. However, you also have to give yourself the chance to "steep."

If you let yourself lean into it, whether it is to scream into a pillow or have an ugly cry, when the emotion is FULLY released, and you have "steeped" long enough, there is suddenly the space to think more clearly and the opportunity to learn something.

Just as with making a good cup of tea, like the tea bag that has steeped long enough, the emotion is ready to be discarded.

If you allowed 5 percent more space to sit with uncomfortable emotions, how would you be able to show up differently?

FOUNDATIONS

Live with compassion. Work with compassion. Die with compassion. Meditate with compassion. Enjoy with compassion. When problems come, experience them with compassion.
THUBTEN ZOPA RINPOCHE

FOUNDATIONS ARE INTERESTING. Some homes are built on a slab, others have crawl space foundations, and then there are basement foundations.

Slab foundations are among the cheapest and most common types. They are popular among homeowners because of the price. The downside of the slab, however, is that, because all the plumbing is underground and dependent on someone being able to break through the concrete, repairs can be expensive. Also, there is minimal protection from bad weather. And of course, proper drainage is important or a huge moisture problem can occur.

Crawl space foundations are elevated a few feet off the ground. Like a slab, a footing is poured, then blocks are laid to create the foundation to support the walls of the structure. This foundation makes it easier to access in case repairs are needed, but once again, there is not much protection from external storms.

And then there is the basement. Most expensive, takes more time, but basements are excellent for anchoring a property to the ground while extending the foundation below the area's frost line, which helps maintain the integrity of the foundation over time. A basement provides more square footage in a home, but you still have to worry about flooding and making sure you have enough light.

Why am I talking about foundations?

In the world of mindsets and self-growth, one's foundation is vital.

As I work with clients, the topics that generally come up are self-esteem and self-confidence. The one topic that I make sure to talk about is self-compassion.

Like foundations, each of these are important and contribute to one's structural integrity. They all help us maintain our base. But there are elements of each that are also important to note.

Self-esteem is like a slab foundation. When self-growth is discussed, oftentimes building self-esteem is the one we hear about the most. It can be a great base. The one thing I have noticed about self-esteem, though, is that it is somewhat based on external comparison. It still has an air of feeling a higher worth based on comparison of our abilities against others' achievements. Many times in an effort to build high self-esteem, we take on this idea that we have to be above average for everything.

Self-confidence can be compared to a crawl space foundation. It is open to outside possibilities. Self-confidence is the belief that we can do something. But we have to watch out for those "I can do this based on what others are achieving around me" thoughts.

Striving for higher self-esteem and self-confidence can sometimes lead to bullying. Why? Because in order to prop oneself up, what ends up happening is the need to take someone else down a notch. These two—self-esteem and self-confidence—are very often dependent on peer approval, on how others will perceive you, and of course success. They increase only when you have proved you are successful.

A basement is the combination of self-esteem, self-confidence, and the third essential prong of self-compassion. Its bottom is deep in the core of who we are, and it rises up with a lot of open space and possibilities.

What is self-compassion?

- Learning to have compassion and love for yourself at all times.
- Learning to be excited for your accomplishments but also compassionate to yourself when things don't go your way.
- Forgiving mistakes and taking a lesson from failures rather than sitting in negativity toward yourself.
- Self-kindness that reminds of us of our common humanity. We are all going through the human experience. At different times, we all struggle, we all fail at something, and we all grow from our mistakes. Learning to do all this gives you such a solid foundation which lots of room to continue growing.

With self-compassion, you may find yourself more motivated. When you practice compassion toward yourself, you are less likely to fear failure. So, you are ready and willing to try.

I am not discounting the importance of self-esteem and self-confidence. They are incredibly important foundations and serve a purpose.

What I do believe, though, is that self-compassion can actually help positively boost self-esteem and self-confidence because when you are no longer cutting yourself down, you are able to see your positives internally rather than basing them on the comparisons of others.

I truly believe each of these three together create self-love which builds resilience and helps one forge ahead as a self-leader.

If you gave yourself 5 percent more self-compassion each day, how would you show up differently?

LOOKING SIDEWAYS MAY BE THE ANSWER

*No matter what happens, it is within my power
to turn it to my advantage.*

EPICTETUS

HAVE YOU EVER done a puzzle and struggled to find a piece that fits?

I was working on a puzzle the other afternoon. I started doing puzzles in my teens to help with anxiety and anxious thoughts. It gave me a way to calm my mind.

Recently while working on a puzzle, I was convinced a certain piece fit into a certain spot. I kept trying and trying, but it just would not fit.

Yet I knew it was meant to be there. I evaluated the puzzle, the picture on the box, and the other pieces, and I just knew this piece was supposed to go there.

I stepped away from the puzzle for a moment.

I allowed the quiet, the space, to dissipate my frustrated feelings until I could see more clearly. I could come up with a next step. Something new to try.

I cocked my head to the side. Looked at the piece form a different angle. And suddenly I knew.

I picked up the piece, turned it ninety degrees—and it fit.

The same can be true of things with which we are struggling.

Sometimes, allowing our mind to quiet by stepping away for a bit helps. Other times it takes a minor mind shift. Think about something with a slight adjustment of ninety degrees. And suddenly things are clearer.

If you knew that whatever way you shifted your thoughts, you were supported, would be more willing to try?

ACKNOWLEDGING THE CRACKS

*It's not the load that breaks you down,
it's the way you carry it.*
Lou Holtz

THE OTHER DAY I was working in my office and sipping tea. My dog was sitting by me when suddenly we heard a shattering sound.

We both jumped up and started searching for what could have caused such a noise. My dog, being the almighty guard dog, quickly ran upstairs to hide in his bed. I kept looking to no avail.

I finished my tea and walked over to the dishwasher to load the dirty mug. When I opened the dishwasher, there was broken glass all over the bottom.

That morning, I had loaded that glass in the dishwasher. I hadn't noticed any cracks or any chips in the glass. But there it was . . . shattered.

As I carefully picked up the pieces, I began to think about all the stress that glass went through. Day in and day out. Hot liquid. Cold liquid. In and out of the dishwasher.

But I never noticed any of its stress, its cracks.

I think sometimes as high-achieving women, we experience something similar. We go through days. We experience highs. We experience lows. But sometimes we don't slow down. We don't recognize when we have "cracks" that need our attention. We just keep "muscling through." And without that time and space, sometimes we fall apart. Sometimes we shatter.

The best gift we can give ourselves is to honor our needs. To give ourselves the gift of self-care and a safe space to feel our feels and release our thoughts.

If you gave yourself just five minutes each day to reflect on how you are feeling, how would you show up differently? What would you see?

MAKING THE TURN

Just keep going. Everybody gets better if they keep at it.
  TED WILLIAMS

THERE ARE MANY four-lane roads where I live, two going each way. Each lane is divided by a white dotted line and a double yellow line in the center dividing the two.

Each morning, there is a line of cars waiting to make a right turn out of our neighborhood onto one of these roads.

Most drivers will wait until the lane closest to them is clear before they go ahead and execute their turn.

This morning I was behind someone who was waiting and waiting. And waiting.

I started to get antsy.

Finally, she made her turn. But instead of turning into the right lane, she turned right into the other lane. The left of the two lanes.

This person waited to make her right turn until both lanes were clear because about a mile up the street, she had to make a left turn.

Why didn't she turn into the right lane closest to her, and then merge into the other lane prior to making her turn?

This got me thinking.

How many of us think that in order to make a change, we have to immediately get into "the correct lane"?

How many of us think we can't get started unless we know we are in a position to succeed?

How many of us delay starting on our path, forgetting that we will slowly inch up to where we want to be?

How many of think it's all or nothing?

What if, just for now, you gave yourself permission to make a slight change? What if you entered the pathway to growth without judging whether you were in the "correct lane" for your journey?

STRIP IT DOWN

*Look within. Within is the fountain of good,
and it will ever bubble up, if thou wilt ever dig.*

Marcus Aurelius

THERE HAS BEEN a lot of road construction around where I live lately. It seems every time I get in the car, at some point during my trip, there will be a flagman holding a big red stop sign. And I will be stopped. With nowhere to go. Simply required to sit and think. Or sit and look around.

Today was no different.

As I sat in my car waiting for the line of traffic to have its turn to go through the intersection, I started to watch what the workers were doing.

They were repaving the road. But they were not just laying down new road. Instead, they were meticulously digging up and removing the old layer of road that had been there for years. It was loud, dusty work. They were sweating bullets. They looked exhausted. But there they were, continuing to dig and remove chunks of asphalt.

I looked down the road to where some other workers had already completely the removal of the old road and now were laying down new asphalt. The asphalt was steaming hot as they laid it down. It looked uncomfortable, but as it began to cool, it settled into place.

This got me thinking.

This is what we go through when faced with transformation.

We have to be ready and willing to peel back old layers of what has been there. Expose the base, which might have been there since we were children. And as we grow, we acquire layers of thoughts and beliefs and behavior patterns that are layered on us. Then one day we realize that the layers have potholes. The layers are no longer serving us. The layers need to be dug out and new layers of thought and beliefs and behavior patterns must be laid down.

It can be tough work to remove the old layers. But when you stick with it, they eventually are chipped away and can be discarded. And as a new layer of mindset is laid down, it can seem uncomfortable at first—"hot," if you will.

But it will start to settle. It will start to feel normal. And then before you know it, you look and there is a smooth road ahead of you.

If you knew that you had a completely safe space to chip away and start removing layers that no longer serve you, how would you proceed?

HOW DO YOU KNOW WHEN IT'S TIME TO LEAP?

Failure is not fatal, but failure to change might be.
DAVID LLOYD GEORGE

THE OTHER MORNING, when I was taking my dog for a walk, there was a loud rustling in the tree behind us.

I stopped to take a look. All the leaves were shaking. And then I saw four squirrels chasing one another up and down the tree trunk. They all ran to the top. And then suddenly one squirrel took an enormous leap off the base of the trunk to a much lower branch.

The branch bobbed up and down once he landed. Once the branch settled down a bit, the squirrel took off again, running and doing his thing.

Watching this, I started to think. How often am I willing to leap like that?

When I look back on decisions or impending possible changes, there have been times when I would be almost be paralyzed. I would get to the edge of the and then stop. The fear of making the wrong decision would prevent me from moving forward. The fear of people judging me for the choice or the change. The fear of letting people down. The fear of "what if it doesn't work out?" The fear that it was the wrong way to go.

As I watched that squirrel, I realized that over time I have come to a place where making a leap doesn't seem as scary. Making the leap now, I know that I am going to land. Good or bad, it will be fine. Because no matter where I land, I will show up and proceed.

If you knew that, no matter what you chose to leap toward, you would be OK, how would you feel?

DIRECTIONALLY CHALLENGED

*Go confidently in the direction of your dreams.
Live the life you've imagined.*
Henry David Thoreau

IF YOU KNOW ME, you know that if you give me directions that include "head east" or "head west," the result will be in a "deer caught in headlights" look from me.

I confess: I am directionally challenged.

That's why I absolutely love my Waze app. Waze will calculate several routes options for me, allow me to pick one, and then if I make an unanticipated turn (aka wrong turn), it will say "Route recalculating."

I don't have to worry about getting lost.

I think in life sometimes we fear change or altering our path because of that very thing . . . the fear of getting lost. The fear that we will make the wrong turn, the wrong decision, and end up being lost. We fear that people will stop loving us. People will be disappointed. People will judge us. So we stop ourselves from proceeding.

But like the Waze app, when you navigate a new path, you will by default recalculate. Why? Because of your inner resilience.

It's there. It may just be hiding.

When you are ready to rediscover and realign with your

resilient self, I am here. I know the path. I get it. I've been there. I am ready to support you in your journey. I invite you to have a simple conversation with me.

Lots of love.

TO BE STUCK OR UNSTUCK

Courage is not the absence of fear, but rather the assessment that something else is more important than fear.
Franklin D. Roosevelt

THE OTHER DAY a friend noticed a baby rabbit that appeared to be stuck in the water spout outside the back of her house. She went over, disassembled the spout and coaxed the little bunny out. It took time and patience. But eventually the little thing came out. It hopped quickly away and carried on with its life.

When she was recounting the story to me, she said, "The funny thing was, he wasn't even stuck. He had just scared himself to the point of being too paralyzed to move. All he needed was knowing that he could get out, and he was fine."

How many times do we think we are stuck, but maybe it's actually fear keeping us paralyzed?

Have you ever been in a situation where you were too scared to make a move, so instead you didn't do anything?

Sometimes we just need a reminder that we are safe. That no matter what we choose to do, we will see the other side. And of course, on the side of fear, fear no longer exists—just a world of possible outcomes.

If you knew that you were 100 percent safe to make a decision, how would you approach things differently?

TO KNOW OR NOT TO KNOW?

Of the gladdest moments in human life ... is the departure upon a distant journey into unknown lands.
RICHARD FRANCIS BURTON

SITTING AT DINNER with some friends and acquaintances the other night, someone was talking about what they do for a living. As she was talking, another woman asked her if she always knew what she wanted to do. The answer was "Yes! I absolutely did!"

The other woman, a mom of teenagers, responded with "Isn't that great? I wish my kids knew what they wanted to do. They seem to be floating through liberal arts right now."

This really stopped me. As I heard the words, "I really wish my kids knew," it was like nails on a chalkboard for me. While I do celebrate those people who actually have a passion for something and truly know what they want, I equally celebrate those who don't. And I honor that uncertainty. Why would we feel bad if our teenager doesn't know what and who they are at the age of eighteen? Why do we feel anxious if they are exploring?

Through working with teens who feel pressure and women who are struggling with not feeling complete with where they are in life, I have seen how "having it all figured out" can actually be being held hostage to expectations in disguise.

They feel afraid to make a change because they are afraid of the social stigma of "changing course," the of fear letting people down. That fear keeps them from moving at all.

Through my work, I provide absolute support and allow space and time for these young adults and women to honor their ideals and values—to follow through with their personal goals without judgment and attachment to what they "should" do. Being able to assist people this way has filled my heart with joy and gratitude—gratitude for being able to witness and be a part of another's personal growth and journey.

It's not about "having all the answers." Instead it's being OK with not knowing. It's about having the willingness to invest time in yourself, to continue on your path, and allow yourself to become.

What if, just for now, you allowed yourself to "not know"? What if you knew that you would be supported and be OK no matter what path you chose—how would you experience life differently?

HOW TIGHT IS YOUR GRIP?

The starting point of all achievement is desire.
Napoleon Hill

DO YOU RECALL learning to drive? Or have you taught your teen to drive recently?

I am in the midst of child number two learning to drive. The other day, as we were moving along, I felt a series of quick, jerky movements in the car. At first, I was not quite sure why, and then I looked over at my son and realized how tightly he was gripping the steering wheel.

Every time he made even the slightest movement of the wheel, the whole car jerked.

This got me thinking. Sometimes in life, when I want something so badly, I will "grip" too tightly or overthink so much that I don't allow enough space for what I want to actually naturally occur.

For instance, one time I was negotiating with a salesperson. I wanted the deal so badly and so quickly. I was "overtrying" or "over-gripping." And before I knew it, the deal fell through.

This can happen when we want to see changes in ourselves. We see the change we want and then we try so hard, move so fast, and when we don't see results right away, we give up. Or we end up hurting ourselves.

But what if we just loosened our grip ever so slightly? What if we just gave ourselves a little space to execute instead of needing to accomplish the change immediately?

Here's to a little looser grip and a little more self-forgiveness.

OUT OF ROUTINE

The world as we have created it is a process of our thinking. It cannot be changed without changing our thinking.

Albert Einstein

RECENTLY, I WAS traveling with my son to a lacrosse tournament. Normally, there is a travel day and then the next day is play day. This time was different. The first game was not until the evening, which gave us time to travel the day of instead.

After the game, when he got off the field, he looked at me and said, "That was awful."

Truthfully, he did not play great. None of his team did. They seemed flat. And one step behind.

I inquired why he thought this was. He said, "I have a routine. And when I am out of it, and don't give myself enough time to regroup, everything is out of sync. I just couldn't get my mind right."

I, too, am extremely routine-oriented. By no stretch am I an athlete, but I like my routine, so when things don't go according to how they normally go, I am out of sync. I feel "out of it." Things seem to be bumpier . . . clunkier. And sometimes things just seem to go wrong.

The way I have started to combat this is that when something out of my normal routine happens, I stop for a moment, pause to take a breath, and acknowledge that this is different. And then I readjust how I am looking at the situation. Instead of thinking This is not how it is supposed to go, I readjust my thought pattern to Interesting, this is new, and my reality shifts.

Learning to move from a place of expectation about how something is supposed to go and into a place of curiosity and knowing that I can handle anything that comes my way has moved me into a place of self-leadership.

Is this easy for those of us who are so used to our routine? Absolutely not. Is it possible? Yes, absolutely.

What if you knew that, no matter what, everything was going to turn out OK? How would you be able to handle changes in your routine?

IF YOU CAN'T DUCT TAPE IT . . .

It is wise to keep in mind that neither success nor failure is ever final.
Roger Babson

IT'S SUMMER. IN my household, that means a lot of travel lacrosse. Recently my son went from a tournament in one state directly to another.

On the first day of the second tournament, I looked down and saw tape around his cleat. After inquiring why, I learned it was because the side of his cleat had separated from the base.

Upon further inspection, I realized that the cleat itself had been glued.

In the past, these types of shoes were sewn together. But in an effort to cut costs and time, someone along the way decided to use the quicker option: glue.

And now the glue had worn out, given way, and the shoe was coming apart.

My son knew he had several more games to play, so he did the next best thing. Duct tape.

Which was a great idea—until it started to rain. The rain and wetness caused the tape to give way. Somehow, my son managed to use the shoe until the end of the day, but that night included a visit to a nearby shoe store to get new cleats.

This whole saga got me thinking.

We, as humans, manage a lot of stressors, and some of us

have a tendency to try to meet expectations. Expectations of others, expectations of ourselves—the shoulds, the ought tos, the never-ending task list.

As we move from thing to thing, we may not take the time for self-care or self-compassion. We do quick fixes and move on. Kind of like using glue on our shoes.

And sometimes, we start to wear down. Sometimes it feels like too much. And sometimes it feels like the glue—or even the "duct tape" that is holding it all together is wearing out too.

What if we went back to the basics? What if instead of using "glue," we gave ourselves some self-love, self-compassion, and self-care, and "sewed" ourselves back together?

When we give ourselves the time and space to feel our feelings but also reset our mindset, we can see that all the times we felt like we were failing or falling were actually growth opportunities on our journey.

We can see how much we have grown, learned, and become stronger. We can see the new seams that have been put into place.

If you knew you had a safe space and were 100 percent supported, would you be able to realign and know that in each step of your journey, you are actually getting stronger, not weaker?

JUDGE JUDY

*Don't get too comfortable with who you are at any given time—
you may miss the opportunity to become who you want to be.*

Jon Bon Jovi

DURING A RECENT flight, I was seated next to a gentleman who was glued to his iPad. I looked over to see what he was watching so intently—it was Judge Judy.

At one point during the flight, I asked him what he liked so much about the show. He said he enjoyed her sarcasm, but he also liked how she was able to solve whatever the problem was between the two people by making a determination of who was right, who was wrong, and in twenty minutes, it was taken care of.

This really got me thinking about quick fixes and someone telling us what to do.

It seems that in today's world, we want things to happen quickly. We want things to change, to be solved, or to be transformed instantaneously. And we love the idea of someone else solving the problem so we don't have to deal with the "icky."

I fall for this myself. After I had each of my babies, I recall going through a stage of wanting someone to tell me the quick way to lose the baby weight and also tell me how to get my newborn to sleep through the night. However, there was no quick fix for the weight. And each child was different. There was no one answer someone could give me. My friends and family supported me as I figured it out.

This is also true for breaking old habits and old ways of thinking and mindsets that no longer serve us. While it would be awesome for someone to give us a magic pill or an answer to change our way of thinking, the truth is that it takes a little commitment. It is also equally true that each of us have to find the answer that works for us. Because we are all unique.

That's why I love what I do. I get to support my clients and assist them to figure out the solutions that work for them. Through my own proven methods of working with individuals, I get to offer a safe, judgment-free space where they can be real. They can feel all the feels. And release thoughts and ideas until they find what works for them. I get to co-collaborate and be there to support and guide. I have the privilege of witnessing these incredible people rediscover and empower themselves while anchoring into their resilience and becoming the self-leader they are meant to be.

No, this work is not done in the time span of an episode of Judge Judy. But "time is not measured by clocks, but by moments." I am honored to be part of those moments.

IT'S JUST HAIR

I can't change the direction of the wind, but I can adjust my sails to always reach my destination.

JIMMY DEAN

MY DAUGHTER HAD decided that she wanted to grow her hair out. Unbeknownst to me at the time, the reason was that she wanted to donate her hair.

At first, we were told that the minimum was ten inches. She had been growing out her hair for months and months, and with the summer looming, she was honestly ready to go ahead and get it cut. She felt a bit defeated.

But then we did some research and found out there were various minimum lengths required. There was not just one length that was "acceptable." Some places would accept eight inches of hair, while others wanted a minimum of ten inches of hair.

Some places would only accept natural hair, while others accepted treated hair, gray hair, or colored hair.

It turns out that each organization has their own way of managing hair donations and creating unique products that serve various people in different communities with unique needs.

We discovered that there really was no one "perfect" way or one "perfect" kind of donation.

This got me thinking about how many times in life we think things have to be one way or it won't work. We think there is a "perfect" way to do something.

And when that "one way" doesn't work, we either feel defeated—or worse yet, we give up.

Where have you struggled with this version of perfectionism?

If you knew that there was no perfect way to do something, but many different ways, how would you show up differently?

TOY STORY 4

I cannot give you the formula for success, but I can give you the formula for failure— which is: Try to please everybody.

HERBERT BAYARD SWOPE

I HAVE BEEN a fan of the *Toy Story* movie franchise since the beginning. Being the mom of five ranging in age from almost eighteen to just turning six, it's no wonder.

So when *Toy Story 4* came out, it was a must-see for me.

This movie hit home. You see, I love Woody. I get him. I resonate with the character. I understand how he operates. The movie opens with a flashback to nine years prior when Woody had the option to leave Andy and go off on an adventure with Bo-Peep. However, he felt obliged to stay with Andy because he felt Andy needed him. Needed him for happiness. Needed him for companionship. Needed him to save him from any sorrow or anxiety.

Woody has a kind soul, and he wants to fix things for his "kids." If they are unhappy or worried, he is there to make them happy, or he finds a way to take care of them. And when he realizes that it is no longer he that makes his new kid, Bonnie, happy, he identifies what does make her happy and then protects it with all his might. He goes out of his way and risks his very self to protect "Forkie" and help him to see his worth and realize how necessary he is to Bonnie's happiness.

Forkie originally thinks he is trash and belongs in the trash. It is Woody who unveils Forkie's worth to him.

When Forkie is lost, Woody ensures that he finds a way to get him back to Bonnie.

As the adventure winds down, Woody is reunited with Bo-Peep and once again has the opportunity to join her and leave his "kid." This time he chooses his own happiness and stays with Bo-Peep and doesn't return to Bonnie.

While the story is really well told and interwoven with much greater care than I am doing here, it reminded me of myself in so many ways.

Perfectionist. People-pleaser. Being all things for others first.

This was soooo me. (And if I am honest, yes, I catch myself slipping there still, because hey, we are all human—and self-growth is a constant journey, not a destination)

But... yeah. I can relate so deeply to Woody. As a young girl, I wanted to please others. I wanted to make sure they were OK. Even if they didn't want to hang out with me, I certainly wanted them to be happy.

As an adult and a perfectionist, I wanted so badly to please others. It felt like a failing if someone was unhappy. Like Woody, I had internalized my obligation and duty to be the one who fixed anything that went wrong. If someone was upset or worried, I tried to carry that for them.

Once I began my transformation, I realized that each of us is responsible for our own happiness. Each of us gets the blessing to carry our own challenges (and it is indeed a blessing, because each challenge offers a new lesson or something to learn). This realization enabled me to actually show up more authentically and be more engaged in life. Like Woody, I began to have a new outlook. A new start. A new way to see the world.

TOY STORY 4

If you or your daughter is struggling with the need to please or the feeling of overwhelm from trying to "fix it," how would you feel if you allowed yourself the ability to let go of just 5 percent of that weight?

TO EACH SHELL HER OWN

We all have our imperfections. But I'm human, and you know, it's important to concentrate on other qualities besides outer beauty.
BEYONCE KNOWLES

RECENTLY ON A vacation to the beach, my youngest and I went searching for shells. We walked up and down the beach and really had a hard time finding some.

We eventually meandered our way back to where her siblings were swimming and just stood, calf-deep in the water, and let the waves come and go.

As we did this, I looked down and noticed . . . a lot of shells. In and out, they came and went with each wave. Shells of different sizes, colors, shapes. Some were intact, some had a hole in the middle, and some were barely recognizable as part of a shell.

As my daughter and I bent down to gather some of these shells, I began to think.

When we were on the search for a perfect shell, we couldn't see any. When we slowed down and just settled ourselves, suddenly we were surrounded by tons of shells.

And then I started to ponder even more. Was there even such a thing as a "perfect shell"? Each one that we picked up was so incredibly interesting. I just knew there was a story behind how it got its shape, color, or hole in the middle.

I started to think about how this is relatable to us as humans.

So many of us strive to be flawless, but what if our flaws are what make us so intriguing? What if the thing we think is our weakness actually makes us unique and memorable? What if our imperfections are what makes us perfectly perfect?

And is it possible that when we allow ourselves to slow down, to let things settle around us, we can ACTUALLY see them more clearly?

So here is a fist bump and high five to all of us imperfect perfects. And I wonder: If you allowed yourself 5 percent more self-compassion, or 5 percent more acceptance of who you are or where you are in life, what would be possible for you to see?

OVER THE RAINBOW

*The way I see it, if you want the rainbow,
you gotta put up with the rain.*
DOLLY PARTON

THE OTHER DAY we had typical afternoon rainstorm. When it was over, as I glanced at the sky, I saw a gorgeous rainbow.

Rainbows always make me smile, and the one I saw did not fail. But as I sat in awe of these colors shining through the cloudy sky, it got me thinking.

The rainbow is made possible through a mix of dark and light.

Just as the rain ends, the dark clouds part ever so slightly to allow for the sun's rays to peek through, hitting off the water droplets to produce this amazing beauty.

As I thought about this, I realized there have been so many times in my own life that I criticize myself for not being happier, cheerier, or simply not being "more put together."

There are those moments when I think I need to have it all figured out. Or I think that somehow I may be letting someone down.

But then I asked myself, if a rainbow which is formed from the mixing of light and dark produces this gorgeous, smiling inducing product . . . what if just for now, we started recognizing that our darker moments mixed with our lighter ones makes us us? And what if we start seeing ourselves as the amazing, smile-inducing humans we are?

BUT THAT'S NOT WHAT THE RECIPE SAYS

When obstacles arise, you change your direction to reach your goal; you do not change your decision to get there.

Zig Ziglar

MY DAUGHTER WANTED to make gluten-free cookies. She had found a recipe online. Of course, we were missing all the butter the recipe called for.

This called for a Google search.

We found that applesauce for butter. With as many kids as I have, there is never a lack of applesauce in the pantry.

My daughter was really worried about changing up the recipe. She kept saying, "That's not what it says. It says you have to use these specific ingredients."

I finally convinced her to give it a try. What was the worst thing that could happen? The cookies don't taste right and we try again?

The whole thing got me thinking.

There are many times in life when we think something has to be done a specific way because of our expectations or because that's what the directions state. And as kids we are taught to always follow directions.

But sometimes, there are other ways to get to an end result rather than one specific path.

Sure, sometimes one path is straighter than another. But sometimes the path that is straight lacks something else.

In this instance, we could have followed the recipe as written. But by changing it up, we allowed for a little more creativity. We got to experience a little more autonomy in how the cookies would turn out. And I may add, they were delicious!

Is there a time when you may have wanted to venture off a scripted path and wondered what might have been if you had?

Have you ever worried about not following directions because you were worried about not meeting expectations or messing something up?

What if you allowed yourself enough space to explore a different way to approach things? What might be possible?

UNEXPECTED GROWTH

Conformity is the jailer of freedom and the enemy of growth.
John F. Kennedy

WALKING ALONG THE greenway the other day, I passed the gate, which is anchored in the ground by cement.

I glanced down and saw this really tall weed growing right out of the cement. At first, I didn't really believe it was growing through the that thick cement, but I took a closer look. And sure enough, it was.

It was so strange. How could a weed find a way to grow through something as thick and non-environmentally friendly to plant growth? And this was not tiny weed, either; it was certainly thriving.

This got me thinking.

I have had many difficult experiences throughout life thus far. I think back to my teen years. There were many times when things happened that did not feel so great.

Social pressure, academic pressure, athletic pressure, and more.

As an adult, there have been other pressures. Taking care of a family, a household, a job, and so on.

And sometimes I have felt overwhelmed, and like I couldn't handle it.

When we experience those tension-filled, tough conditions,

we might think that nothing good will come out of this, or that we just can't get it all done. Some of us who hate to think we are letting others down may even feel like a failure.

But if we step back, every experience gives us the chance to grow. The real questions are: Do we take it? Are we open to it?

As I walked past this weed growing strong and tall through the cement block in the ground, I wondered: If we just gave ourselves just a bit more self-compassion and space to be ourselves, would we see that we are actually growing? If we forgave ourselves, even in tough conditions, would we start to embrace ourselves a bit more?

BOUNDARY BUBBLE

Healing may not be so much about getting better, as about letting go of everything that isn't you—all of the expectations, all of the beliefs— and becoming who you are.

RACHEL NAOMI REMEN

A NEW PUPPY has joined our family, which includes an older dog. Once again, I am right back into the world of housebreaking, teething, teaching a routine, etc. Except this time, the kids are older, so they are actually playing a role in the whole process.

This past weekend at breakfast the puppy climbed up on the kitchen chair while my daughter ate. I quickly corrected the dog. My daughter was aghast. "Mom, don't be mean. It's so cute how he climbs up to see me."

I reminded her: "Puppies grow bigger. They soon can reach the table. And if we don't teach him boundaries of what he can and cannot do, he will misbehave and start stealing your food right off the table."

This got me thinking about boundaries.

As a people-pleasing perfectionist myself, I know how hard it is to set boundaries. We tend to think, Oh, that's mean or They will be mad at me, all in the name of trying to meet someone else's expectations or trying to do everything for everyone.

This can be difficult to confront when you have not set boundaries in the past and you realize that without them, you are carrying around the weight of the world. People get used to being a certain way. You get used to you in a certain way. And so it is scary to think of actually resetting.

Likewise, in life, even when we set boundaries with people and in relationships, sometimes they are tested. And it's up to us to ask ourselves, "What are we willing to accept?"

We need to learn to give ourselves permission to set boundaries and to decide what we want. Otherwise that feeling of overwhelm or frustration can start to creep in.

Back to the dogs for a second...

The older dog knows the boundaries we have set in the kitchen. And as time has passed, he has started to push that boundary. He creeps into the kitchen now. He lays his head on the kitchen table as we eat. And unless we enforce the boundary with him, he also tends to grab food right off someone's plate.

This is true in life. Even when you have set boundaries, you have to honor them and check on them regularly. At times you may find you need or want to change them. And that's OK. Other times you will want them to stay the same. Also OK.

What's important is to honor yourself. Honor what it is you want and what it is you are willing to accept.

If you allowed yourself permission to set some boundaries in your life, how would you be able to show up differently?

DOES THE SHOE FIT?

Don't wait. The time will never be just right.
NAPOLEON HILL

I CANNOT EVEN begin to the count the number of times I have read and seen Cinderella. To think a whole marriage and life was based on finding the person whose foot fit into one particular shoe!

But it's true. Finding a shoe that fits your foot perfectly is difficult. I cannot count the number of times that I have tried on a pair of shoes in the store only to get them home, put them on, and then realize that they don't feel right. They pinch, or maybe they are too loose.

I have recently been wearing the new shoe that advertises a lot on the internet: Rothy's. I find them super comfortable. They bend with my foot, they are soft, they can be casual, and they can be dressed up. Best of all, they are washable.

It's funny, though. People ask me about them all the time. And I always find myself offering the caveat that "they work for me, but shoes are a pretty personal thing."

This happened again recently, and I started think, Why do I do that?

I realized that the right fit is not only related to shoes. It happens all the time. Especially in service-related industries.

For instance, one of my daughters absolutely loves a

particular hairdresser, while my other daughter, not so much. One mom and dad may swear by a pediatrician's office, while others cannot stand that particular office.

This happens with coaches too. Let's be honest—there are a lot to choose from. But not all people resonate with one another. It is so important to find the right fit.

When I work with someone, I always start with a conversation where we can explore what's going on and what that person is looking for. It is important to me to really take the time to learn about the person and see if we are a fit for each another.

I pride myself on truly and wholeheartedly holding a safe space for my clients, a place where it is OK for them to challenge their thoughts or mine. A place for them to fully embrace the ability to be true to who they are.

When you are ready, feel free to reach out.

BLISTERS GET YOU READY

There is no coming to consciousness without pain.
CARL JUNG

MY OLDEST DAUGHTER is in a professional ballet training program. She has been dancing since she was two years old. In the beginning, however, the dancers wear very soft slippers. As they get more advanced, they eventually transition to pointe shoes.

Each new pair of pointe shoes needs to be broken in, just as when my daughter takes time off, her feet need to be broken in again.

What this means is that she comes home with bloody toes and bloody popped blisters all over her feet.

It's honestly kind of gross. And I end up buying boxes and boxes of band aids.

But this is part of the journey.

With each blister, her feet "learn."

And while the bruises are tough, she continues. Because each bruise teaches something. It's all a learning process.

The other night, as I watched her soak her feet, I just felt for her.

And then I started to think.

This is kind of like our journey through life. As we engage, as we take our journey, there are bumps and bruises. But with each one, we learn. And if we take what we learn and move forward, it is not in vain.

And when we need to rest and "soak our feet," or in some cases let our minds rest, we do that. And then we show up the next day. Because. We. Are. Resilient.

As it has been said time and again by various people, including Tony Robbins and Sean Stephenson: "Life is happening for us, not to us."

If you knew that every bruise you felt along your journey was teaching you something, how would you be able to show up differently each day?

BUILDING BLOCKS

The one thing that you have that nobody else has is you.
Your voice, your mind, your story, your vision.
So write and draw and build and play and dance
and live as only you can.

Neil Gaiman

THE OTHER DAY my daughter was building a castle with her building blocks. As she was working, the blocks kept tumbling down.

She got extremely frustrated.

I heard myself telling her, "It's going to be OK. Just start again."

As the words tumbled out of my mouth, I actually heard myself.

And it got me thinking.

Being "type A" and working with a lot of high achievers, I have seen this time and again—the anxiety that comes with wanting to control a situation and feeling like it is all crumbling down, with no control to fix it.

I've seen the stress and worry that comes with the feeling that, as it all crumbles, you may be thought of as a failure. Or judged for a failing project. Or for letting someone down. The list goes on.

But what if we breathe for a moment . . . and realize that

things are going to fall apart or seemingly crumble, and . . .
What have you always done?
You've showed up and started again. Block by block. You have built your tower or your castle again.

If you knew without a doubt that no matter what crumbled around you, there was no shame or guilt, just the chance to build again, how would you show up differently?

IT WAS ALWAYS BURNING

I am building a fire, and every day I train, I add more fuel. At just the right moment, I light the match.

Mia Hamm

THINK ABOUT THE times you've sat back and watched a fire burn.

Recently, as the kids were roasting marshmallows, I sat back and watched the fire burn through the logs. I watched as the flame would appear in one place, then disappear only to reappear in a different location, with a brighter and taller flame in a different spot on the log.

This got me thinking and reflecting.

In a recent conversation with a client, we were discussing a project she was working on and then abruptly abandoned. She had started to feel overwhelmed and worried about failing and eventually just stopped all together.

As she and I talked, what became apparent was the overwhelm of one thing not going the way she planned, which resulted in the feeling of not good enough and being worried about being judged. So she ended up just letting the whole thing die out.

We talked about giving herself some space and compassion. We painted a picture of what that would look like. Instead of viewing things that did not go the way she envisioned as failures or mistakes, she started to see them as learning opportunities. We explored how she could move past the need to please others and looking to them for their approval.

She realized that if one path did not seem to work, she could try another. All that was needed was her willingness to go there.

This was just like the flame I was watching.

As the fire burned, the flame could not burn through one piece of the wood. Maybe it was wet. Maybe it was too charred, or not charred enough. Whatever the reason, the fire itself moved along, and the flame came back bigger and stronger . . . just in another place.

As humans we have passions, desires, things we want to do and be—fires that burn.

What if we give ourselves the grace we deserve to try one path, and when it doesn't work the way we want, we find another?

If you knew that you could not fail, how would you show up differently when working on projects or in relationships?

WALKING ON EGGSHELLS

> *Your pain is the breaking of the shell*
> *that encloses your understanding.*
> KHALIL GIBRAN

WELL, NOT REALLY walking on eggshells . . . just cracking them.

This morning I was making eggs for breakfast. I cracked the eggs and placed them in the pan. As they sat there, I realized I had so many options. Do I make scrambled? An omelet? Sunny-side up? Fried? The list went on. (I actually made scrambled because they are the easiest for me.)

But this got me thinking.

Sometimes people can be like eggs. Think about the way we carry eggs so delicately so as not to crack them. Some of us get bogged down with keeping up with "all the things," and we worry about "cracking." Because if we crack, or even worse, if someone sees a crack, it would be the equivalent of failing.

But here's the thing. Just like the eggs, when we are cracked open, our vulnerabilities exposed from beneath "our shell," given time, space and support, there is a world of growth and opportunity ahead of us.

It's up to us what we decide.

If you knew that you were completely safe to shed light on your vulnerabilities and stressors, what would be possible for you?

THE BLIND SPOT

The traveler sees what he sees,
the tourist sees what he has come to see.

Gilbert K. Chesterton

TEACHING SOMEONE ELSE to drive is eye-opening.

During a driving lesson with my son, I had to remind him to check his blind spot. He had no idea what I was referring to at first, but then I explained how it's the part you cannot see with your mirrors and you have to actually peek over your shoulder.

This got me thinking.

There are times when I am barreling ahead with the tasks on my list and the things I want to accomplish, and I forget to take a quick look around.

It's as if I have blinders on.

The feeling of "let me just get this done, and then all will be OK" and then that task is done—and lo and behold, a new one appears, and the thought recycles "let me just get this done and all will be OK," and on and on.

It's that dang blind spot. The area we just keep ignoring. If we don't look over that shoulder of ours and see what's there, it can wreak havoc.

If in that blind spot, it is time to rest and recharge, we need to see it.

If in that blind spot, it is time to let our emotions be, we need to see it.

If in that blind spot, there is more self-compassion, we need to see it.

What are you not seeing? If you had someone to support you, what would be possible for you to see?

THE MOTH VERSUS THE BUTTERFLY

Winners compare their achievements with their goals, while losers compare their achievements with those of other people.

Nido R. Qubein

THE OTHER DAY I was in the parking lot and saw a moth on the ground. At first, I did not even realize it was a moth. I had always assumed that moths were pesky creatures that flew around at night. I assumed they were all white or gray in color and had no real markings on them.

They were plain compared to a butterfly, which I saw as a beautiful and delicate creature that would quietly float through the air.

As I took a closer look at this moth, I realized that he was larger than I ever knew a moth could get. And his markings were actually quite intricate. He wasn't just a plain white or gray color.

This got me thinking.

Why would I compare a moth to a butterfly and think that one was better than the other?

How often do we compare things in life and assume that one is better than the other?

How often do we compare ourselves to others and think how much better someone else is at something, or how much prettier or smarter?

And what happens when we live in this box of comparison?

When we compare, we can get lost in being the same as others and fitting in. Just like my comparison of the moth to the butterfly. I thought one was prettier than the other. One was more delicate than the other. One was nicer than the other.

Comparison robs us of seeing and realizing the uniqueness we have that benefits our community and the world.

We miss out on so much beauty, originality, and creativity.

It happens in so many areas of life: parenting, work, relationships.

But what if, just for now, you allowed yourself to step outside of the "norm" and be a little different?

LOST IN THE MAZE

Obstacles can't stop you. Problems can't stop you. Most of all, other people can't stop you. Only you can stop you.
Jeffrey Gitomer

WE WERE OUT to dinner recently, and my daughter was given a kid's menu with a maze on it. She quickly grew frustrated because she could not figure how to get from the beginning to the end.

I jumped into action because I actually love solving puzzles—so I was eager to bestow my wisdom. I explained how I have always solved these mazes by starting at the end and moving backward.

She quickly caught on and figured out how to solve the puzzle.

This got me thinking.

Many times in life we face a dilemma, a problem, or a "puzzle." When we look at it, it feels overwhelming, and we want to solve it immediately.

We either don't know how to solve it and stay paralyzed—or we start, but what we try doesn't seem to be working, and then we get stuck.

What if we don't know exactly how we are supposed to get to our goal, but choose to look at it from a different perspective?

What if we look at the goal, and then work backward?

The last piece of advice I gave my daughter was this: "When working a maze like this, use a pencil, and if you go the wrong way, just erase it!"

When we are trying to solve a problem in life, what if we used self-compassion as though it were a pencil? What if we forgave ourselves? What if we reminded ourselves that we are doing the best we can? And then, what if we moved forward?

If you knew that every step you take on your journey in life is where you are meant to be, how would you be able to approach problems differently?

AUTHENTIC . . . ONE OF TODAY'S BUZZWORDS

"Real isn't how you are made," said the Skin Horse. "It's a thing that happens to you. When a child loves you for a long, long time, not just to play with, but really loves you, then you become Real."

"Does it hurt?" asked the Rabbit.

"Sometimes," said the Skin Horse, for he was always truthful. "When you are Real, you don't mind being hurt."

"Does it happen all at once, like being wound up," he asked, "or bit by bit?"

"It doesn't happen all at once," said the Skin Horse. "You become. It takes a long time. That's why it doesn't often happen to people who break easily, or have sharp edges, or who have to be carefully kept. Generally, by the time you are Real, most of your hair has been loved off, and your eyes drop out, and you get loose in the joints and very shabby. But these things don't matter at all, because once you are Real, you can't be ugly, except to people who don't understand."

FROM *THE VELVETEEN RABBIT* BY MARGERY WILLIAMS

MY COACHING PRACTICE is based on the concept of realigning with and rediscovering your authentic self . . . hence the term I created: AuthenticMe®.

However, in an age where it seems there are buzzwords, the words themselves get tired and overused—in essence they lose some of their impact and meaning.

Brené Brown defines authentic as the daily practice of letting go of who we think we're supposed to be and embracing who we are.

"Letting go of who we think we are supposed to be" hits in on the head for me.

High achievers and those who feel compelled to try to do it all, and be everything for everyone, never dropping "a ball," consistently muscling through, no matter what, many times battle this very thing. It's all about learning to be yourself, without the need for external validation, without the need of fulfilling someone else's expectation. It's learning to drop any expectations you hold as to who you ought to be because there is an underlying feeling that who you are is not good enough—or simply put, enough.

Being authentic is a choice. A choice to show up as you. A choice to be unapologetically you.

In a world where comparisons are rampant, this can be so difficult. I get it.

We worry about letting others down, about being judged, about messing up, about not measuring up to others. We think it's about how we look on the outside rather than the core of who we are on the inside.

However, when we allow ourselves to let go of the "shoulds" and allow for our vulnerability and our "real self" to shine through, that transparency makes us able to really be present in our lives. To really and truly connect with others who are meant to connect with us. And that connection with others is what makes it possible to really live in joy.

If you knew that you were 100 percent accepted as the true you, how would you show up differently in your life?

PIV...OOOT!

To improve is to change; to be perfect is to change often.
WINSTON CHURCHILL

I GREW UP in the era of Friends. One of the most memorable scenes is when Chandler and Ross are trying to move a couch up a staircase. Ross's character keeps yelling "Pivot! Pivot! Piv...ooot!

This scene popped into my head the other day as I heard someone say the word pivot. I found myself chuckling, and then I started to think about the word a bit more—and the concept of pivoting.

When we are little, we are asked a lot "What do you want to be when you grow up?"

When we are in our late teens and early twenties, we choose a major. Then as we grow, some of us get married, we have kids, we make "our plan."

But...what if...we want to...pivot?

What if that was actually OK? What if, instead of thinking it was a failing or a rejection of someone or something, we embraced it? What if we looked at it as growth?

If you allowed yourself the permission to pivot, what would change for you?

IT MAY NOT BE SHORTER

All comes at the proper time to him who knows how to wait.
St. Vincent de Paul

I SPEND A lot of time in the car, running from one part of town to the other. Today was no different. And once again, I came to this particular intersection that is ALWAYS congested.

I thought to myself, I can get around this traffic. I'll just go the "back way."

I proceeded along. I got to the final red light that would put me back on the road I would have originally ended up on, only to see cars that I was also originally behind drive past me as I waited to execute my turn.

And then I thought . . .

Here I was trying to beat the traffic. Trying to get ahead. Trying to cut down on my travel time. And in the end, the people I had been behind got there at the same time I did.

What did I gain?

All I cut out was standing still and thinking I wasn't getting anywhere.

And it hit me: How often do we think that we aren't moving, aren't getting anywhere, but in fact we are just where we are supposed to be—and given time, we will move just as we are supposed to?

In your own life, how often do you think:

- I am not getting anywhere.
- I am stuck.
- Things aren't moving fast enough.

What if you knew, without a doubt, that you were going to end up exactly where you were meant to be? Would you be able to be more present in your daily life? Would you enjoy the ride more?

I NEVER NOTICED THAT BEFORE . . .

To acquire knowledge, one must study; but to acquire wisdom, one must observe.

MARILYN VOS SAVANT

THE OTHER DAY we were driving through a neighborhood that we have gone through more times than I can count. As we passed one property, I said out loud, "I have never noticed that house before. It's so pretty."

I admired the house as we went by, and then it got me thinking.

There have been so many times when I have seen something, but not observed it.

> Holmes: "You see, but you do not observe. The distinction is clear. For example, you have frequently seen the steps which lead up from the hall to this room."
> Watson: "Frequently."
> Holmes: "How often?"
> Watson: "Well, some hundreds of times."
> Holmes: "Then how many are there?"
> Watson: "How many? I don't know."
> Holmes: "Quite so! You have not observed. And yet you have seen. That is just my point."
>
> FROM *THE ADVENTURES OF SHERLOCK HOLMES* BY ARTHUR CONAN DOYLE

We go through our "every day." We are so used to the scripts we have given ourselves, our thought patterns, our behavior patterns, that we can miss things.

We get so caught up in "nexting" and juggling all "the things" that sometimes we don't "observe" the feelings or the emotions we have.

And when we fail to actually observe, we drain ourselves.

If you knew that it was completely safe to slow down and observe what you feel and what you think, what do you think you would see? What would be possible for you?

HOT COFFEE

We accept the love we think we deserve.
STEPHEN CHBOSKY

THE OTHER MORNING as we all were getting ready for the day, I looked around and noticed that everyone had gotten their cup of coffee and I had yet to fill mine.

I went ahead and filled my cup.

Just as I did, emptying the coffee pot, my spouse mentioned that he needed more coffee for his mug because he had a long drive ahead of him.

Without missing a beat, I offered to give him some of mine, as I had a full travel mug.

This got me thinking.

Had I not had a full cup, I would have had nothing to offer.

This is true of self-care too. It's when we don't take care of our needs and offer ourselves some compassion and self-kindness that we remain running on "empty." And then we can't REALLY show up for others if they need us.

If you were to just allow yourself 5 percent more care to "fill your cup up" on a daily basis, how would you feel? How would you show up differently?

DENSE FOG ADVISORY

When you're first thinking through an idea, it's important not to get bogged down in complexity. Thinking simply and clearly is hard to do.
RICHARD BRANSON

WHILE GETTING READY, I heard an alarm on my phone. I have a weather app that alerts me with any advisories for our area. Turns out a dense fog advisory warning had been issued.

As I drove the morning carpool run, there was definitely thick fog in the area. I could only see a few yards in front of me. So that's what I did—crept along a few yards at a time.

As I dropped the kids off, I started to think.

The ride to school took a little bit longer, but we were not late. The pathway was not clear for miles, but I was able to see a few yards a t time, and still managed to get there safely.

This is somewhat true of difficulties in life along our journey. Sometimes the overwhelm can feel so great. Sometimes we cannot see a clear path to get to where we thing we "ought to be."

But what if we give ourselves grace to slow our pace down a bit?

Grace to recognize we can only see a couple inches in front of us. And that's OK.

During those times, we just take those smaller steps in

front of us. And we keep going. And eventually we get to exactly where we are meant to be. Safely. Authentically.

What if you knew that it was completely safe to slow down and take your time? How would you be able to handle those moments of overwhelm differently?

THE BALLOON

*A certain amount of opposition is a great help to a man.
Kites rise against, not with, the wind.*

Lewis Mumford

RECENTLY WE PURCHASED a helium balloon at the store for my daughter.

She was so excited and happy. When we left the store, it was kind of windy. It was blustery, in fact.

She held on as tight as she could manage to the string, determined to get this balloon into the car. She was trying so hard to control the balloon, as it shifted one way and then the other, the wind knocking it around.

Eventually the knot tying the string to the balloon loosened just enough, and away the balloon floated.

We stood and watched it.

It rose.

And rose.

Higher.

Higher still.

Upward.

It was not carried by the wind, but instead it just kept rising higher and higher. The helium in the balloon was enough to fight against the wind and lift it off up into the sky.

I started to think.

I have been known to be like my daughter, holding on tightly and trying to control what's about to happen while life has been blustery, throwing twists and turns like the wind.

But over time, realizing that maybe I could be more like the balloon. Cutting ties with the string and using its own inner being to rise above the winds. To rise above what was trying to whisk it away.

Allowing ourselves to be free from the "ought tos" or the "shoulds" can set us free. Allowing our own inner intuition, our own mindsets and behaviors can help carry us to where we want to go.

So, if just for now, you allowed yourself to let go of some of those "ought tos," would you be freer to rise to who you really are?

I HAVE BERMUDA GRASS

You are what you think about.
GAUTAMA BUDDHA

MY FRIEND WAS telling me the other day about her Bermuda grass. She was telling me how the grass would grow into the mulch, and it looked awful.

She would sit for hours trying to pull weeds. It was a struggle because the grass was so strong and so rooted in the ground.

After two years went by, she decided to try using a guard around her mulch beds. But the grass just grew under the barrier and still invaded her mulch bed.

Then someone suggested she try weed killer. She sprayed it. And let it sit for a few days before trying to address it again.

When she returned to pull the weeds, they simply came right out. No more struggle.

This got me thinking.

The stories we tell ourselves and the negative, stuck thought cycles we sometimes enter are just like those weeds. They are deep rooted and strong.

They find ways to get around little barriers we try to put up. For example, we may think, Oh, I will just think positive, and this will get better. But the negativity still finds a way, and we still feel stuck.

However, maybe, when we feel this "stuckness," this negativity, these emotions that don't feel so good, we need to see the emotion or the thought. Observe it. Let is rise and crest. And once it has, when we return to address it, it is not so hard to remove—or better yet, we can look at the situation differently.

If you knew that your thoughts were only there for a short time and would eventually settle, would you be able to shift your perspective more easily?

WHERE'S MY CHARGER?

Never mistake activity for achievement.
JOHN WOODEN

I AM ONE of those weird people that really never likes the battery on my phone to get below 50 percent. It seems like as soon as it does, the rest of the battery just disappears within the blink of an eye.

I know it's odd. Why does it bother me so much to have the battery on my phone drained?

Well, first of all, I hate to see that flashing red graphic that pops up with the drained battery. I also have absolutely no patience to wait for it to charge.

Do you know what I mean?

It seems like that drained battery takes forever to actually recharge.

So I am usually very careful and make sure I routinely charge my phone.

But how many of us do that for ourselves?

I have definitely run myself around to the point of exhaustion, either physical or mental, because I "had to muscle through" or "there was no time to rest" or I thought it would be considered weak or slacking if I didn't have one hundred things to do on my plate AND I accomplished them all.

Sound familiar by chance?

Why is it that we take better care of charging our phones than we do our bodies and our minds?

When we let ourselves get so depleted, the time it takes to recover is that much greater, both physically and mentally.

If you knew that slowing down to recharge yourself would actually allow you to be more present in your daily life or even possibly accomplish more, what are some ways you would recharge?

HAUNTED HOUSES

*If you're never scared or embarrassed or hurt,
it means you never take any chances.*

ROSALYN DREXLER

IT'S THAT TIME of the year.

Haunted houses. Scary corn mazes.

My kids are all about them. Knowing full well they will be scared crazy but all the while asking to go . . . begging to go.

This got me thinking.

Why would they seek out the fright? Why is it that people want to go into a building when they know it will include frightening screams and such?

What I realized is that our consciousness is aware of the scariness, but it is equally aware that it will be over in a specified time. We also know that we will find the "fun" in the weird, random, crazy things that come out.

But in life, sometimes we let fear get in the way of moving forward. Doing something new or something we are not sure we can succeed at can be scary. So we back away from it. We don't engage.

Maybe it's because we don't know what things will come at us.

Maybe it's because we don't know how long it will last.

Or maybe we don't trust that we will come out the other

end. Or better yet, we have told ourselves the story that unless we succeed, we "won't survive."

What if, when something new, something out of your comfort zone, appears, you looked at it more like a haunted house? You don't know what will come at you. But you know you will find the fun. You don't know how long the challenge will last, but you do know that you will come out on the other side.

If you knew that, no matter what, you would be OK and you would learn something, would you be less scared to try something out of your comfort zone?

I CAN SEE CLEARLY NOW

We don't see things as they are, we see them as we are.
Anais Nin

THE OTHER DAY was my yearly visit to the eye doctor. Without my glasses or contacts, I cannot see past a mere inch or two in front of my face. So unlike other doctors' visits, I actually look forward to the eye doctor.

Every time I leave that office, I see more clearly than when I walked in. I can suddenly see the details of the leaves on threes rather than mere outlines. And that is such a thrilling and invigorating feeling! In all honesty, it is empowering.

This got me thinking.

We all experience the world differently, and we all see things differently.

For instance, remember that picture of the dress that caused such a stir on social media?

Some saw one set of colors; some saw another.

We all see things through our own lens. And when our mindset shifts, the way we see things can shift. Just like getting a new pair of glasses or contacts. We could can see things more clearly ... or at least differently.

If you had the support and the space to clean your "lens," what do you think you would see as possible for you?

THE DIRT IS SOMETIMES MORE THAN JUST DIRT

Sitting quietly, doing nothing, Spring comes, and the grass grows, by itself.
MATSUO BASHO

IT'S SCIENCE FAIR project time. This year it's all about what type of "watering" liquid enables the fastest plant growth.

As I helped my son plant all the seeds into the dirt, I remembered that Thích Nhât Hạnh quote, "No mud. No lotus flower."

Here we were planting the seeds. All we could see is dirt. But knowing that if we take care, if we water, the seeds will grow.

This got me thinking.

Life throws so many curves at us. There are times when we can feel overwhelmed, stress-ridden, or overrun with anxiety. It feels dark. If feels heavy.

But if we take time . . . if we give space . . . if we take care of ourselves, there will be growth.

If you knew that even the darkest of moments or heaviest of thoughts would pass and you would grow, how would you show up differently each day?

HOW THIN IS THE BUTTER?

*Love the moment and the energy of that moment
will spread beyond all boundaries.*

CORITA KENT

OUT AT DINNER the other night, the server brought a basket of bread to the table. And honestly, I cannot resist.

I took a piece of bread out of the basket, grabbed a pat of butter and began spreading it. It was kind of clumpy and only in one spot of the bread. I tried harder to get the butter to spread evenly.

I finally was able to spread the butter across the entire piece of bread, trying to reach each inch of it.

As I did this, I began to think.

As a mother and wife, how often do I try to spread my energy and attention evenly, to reach every single area of my life?

How often do I think that if I don't get to everything on my daily to-do list, or give my all to every aspect of my life, I have dropped the ball?

How thin do I spread myself by doing so?

How thin do I spread my energy?

What if instead of focusing on spreading my energy evenly across everything, I gave myself grace to be "clumpy"? To put energy in one or two things but not think I have to do it all—and do it all at once?

Does this sound at all familiar?

If you gave yourself just 5 percent more grace to not spread yourself so thin, what would be possible?

I SEE THE TOP

It does not matter how slowly you go as long as you do not stop.

CONFUCIUS

THIS PAST SUMMER we visited one of the lighthouses on the North Carolina coast. We decided to climb to the top, step after step. As we climbed, there were spots to stop and to look out small windows.

Since we had our littles with us, with their shorter legs, we chose to stop at each "break area." It was breathtaking, with each window offering us a different view of the ocean on one side and the sound on the other.

When we made it to the top, it was even more spectacular. All the vantage points we had seen along the way added up to this gorgeous view from the top.

I thought about this climb afterward.

If we had not had the littles with us, I may have been tempted to just keep climbing to the top. Without slowing down. Without taking in the views along the way.

Sure, the view from the top would have still been pretty. But what made it even more breathtaking was having had the chance to see little snippets along the way.

It's kind of like life. When we are so super focused on the end result, sometimes we forget to take in the smaller things along the way. We miss the smaller lessons, the smaller "views."

Maybe it's not so much about the getting to the top—maybe it's more about the climb.

Knowing that you would get to your goal—whether you sprinted straight there or took smaller more deliberate, more aware steps along the way—would you possibly enjoy it more? Would it allow you to be more present in the moment? When you got to the goal, would it feel different?

BEHIND THE SCENES

*Mistakes are always forgivable,
if one has the courage to admit them.*
Bruce Lee

A MOVIE WE watched the other day had bloopers at the end while the credits were running.

I love to watch the bloopers.

It makes me laugh. Not at anyone in particular, and not at anyone for messing up. It just is fun to see these polished actors and actresses being "normal." Tripping over their words like the rest of us do. Not knowing what they are "supposed to say."

It acts as a reminder that even "if" there was a perfect script to read from, deviations from it still occur.

This got me thinking.

Why is it so easy for me to laugh and find the humor in the miscues the actors make while making a movie, and yet I take so hard the small missteps I sometimes make in daily life? The ones I have a hard time forgiving myself for?

What if instead of looking at our missteps, we looked at them as "whoopsie-daisies"?

What if we just didn't take each misstep so seriously? What if we gave ourselves the same grace we give "bloopers"?

If we didn't take ourselves so seriously and saw the fun in things a bit more, what would be possible?

WHAT DOES THE END SAY?

Happiness depends upon ourselves.
ARISTOTLE

Recently a client of mine was telling me how she cannot read a book without looking at the ending. Not knowing if the books ends with a "happy ending" raises her anxiety.

I inquired further.

It turns out that the issue at hand was not liking the conflict in the book. She likes to "get through it quick" and get to the other side.

This really got me thinking.

In relationships this happens all the time. Take the parent and child relationship as an example. There are times that parents don't want to create conflict, and so they avoid the possibility of "saying the wrong thing" and therefore don't address concerns or issues. They worry about setting off a chain reaction of conflict, and that fear keeps them silent.

And when we find ourselves in conflict, we often just want to get through it quickly. We want to skip all the "messy stuff" and just get to the other side.

But when you skip the middle, you miss the growth. When we bring home our newborns, all we really want is for them to sleep through the night. We want to get to the other side of those sleepless nights.

But when we stop and think about it, those sleepless nights offer a lot of bonding time with our child.

While conflict is not fun, just as being overly tired in the middle of the night is not fun, it offers a chance to learn, to challenge our ideas, and to possibly grow. If we "just skip all that," we miss out.

If you knew that going through the uncomfortable would actually make you stronger, how would you approach the "messy" differently?

BACKDRAFT

An airplane takes off against the wind, not with it.
Henry Ford

ONE NIGHT WE had a fire burning in the firepit. As I sat watching the fire, it started to fade. We blew on it, and it reignited.

Backdraft—not exactly an explosion, but with the added oxygen, the extra air, the fire certainly began to burn heavier, brighter, and stronger.

This got me thinking.

There have been times when I am feeling sad about something. And I have tried to muscle through . . . because that's what some of us perfectionists do . . . we don't like to admit that we need help.

Then someone comes along and asks, "Is everything OK?"

Boom! Backdraft. The floodgates open.

The tears begin to fall. To stream down our cheeks. And the emotions are released.

By releasing them, they are able to rise and crest, and we can move forward. Much like the way the oxygen ignites the fire. It burns and does its thing, and then it peters out.

When we hide the emotions or push them down, they are left unresolved.

But when we allow them out, to be without judgment, we can shift and move forward.

We can practice observation and compassion.

What if instead of hiding emotions or muscling through, we gave ourselves the grace to let them out—how would our mindset shift?

BUNCHED-UP SOCKS

*Anyone can hide. Facing up to things,
working through them, that's what makes you strong.*

Sarah Dessen

I WALK AROUND like everything is fine. But deep down, inside my shoe, my sock is sliding off.

Something similar happened to me the other day. Except this time, I had put on a pair of barn socks. These socks are a bit thicker, and sometimes they bunch up at the toe area. They felt a bit bunchy, but I was running late, so I threw on my boots and figured it would work itself out.

Instead, however, the bunched-up sock ended up causing a blister.

Had I just slowed down for an extra minute in the morning, took off my boot, and rearranged my sock, I could have avoided the bigger issue I now had—a really annoying, and painful blister.

This got me thinking.

There are times in our everyday life when we feel like something is off; we know something is not quite working for us. But we muscle through.

We muscle through because either we think if we slow down and address it, we will "run out of time," or we simply resign ourselves to thinking, That's just the way it is, and I'll get used to it.

But here's the thing.

When we don't address the thing that doesn't feel good or even hurts a bit, we make it worse. Sometimes, slowing down and addressing what isn't working can actually help us move forward.

Sure, slowing down or stopping for a minute may not feel so great in the moment. But once the issue is addressed and you can move forward, suddenly it feels better. Lighter.

If you knew that stopping and addressing the thing that isn't working could actually make the journey less painful in the long run, in what way or ways would you slow down?

ZIPPERS

No matter who you are, no matter what you did, no matter where you've come from, you can always change, become a better version of yourself.

Madonna Ciccone

HAVE YOU EVER had a zipper that has come off its track?

The other day a friend was wearing a pair of boots. She showed me how the zipper had become misaligned from one of those tiny brass pieces near the bottom of the zipper.

As the day wore on the zipper gave way, until eventually, the entire zipper had separated.

A small little piece in a train of pieces that are assembled to work together that had come off its track eventually led to the whole thing separating.

This got me thinking.

I realized that one piece in a system being off can really have a domino effect. This happens with our behavior patterns. When one piece of our "system" stops working the way it should, the whole system can come crashing down, leaving us feeling exposed and isolated.

That's when self-compassion plays a huge role. Remembering we are not alone. Remembering our common humanity.

Once the zipper had come apart on her boot, there was

not much she could do for that particular zipper. However, she realized she could seek someone to help her fix it or replace it.

In a similar way, when we recognize that a behavior pattern may not be serving us anymore, it might be time to seek support to help shift it. It might be time to give yourself the time and space to see what no longer serves you and what would serve you better.

If you gave yourself 5 percent more space to shift your unwanted behavior patterns, the ones taking you off track, what new possibilities might open up for you?

THE NEW OWNER

*Your life does not get better by chance,
it gets better by change.*

JIM ROHN

I HAVE BEEN visiting a certain coffee shop for years. It's always been a nice place to sit, drink coffee, grab a snack, work, and meet with people.

A little bit ago the shop was sold, and new owners took over.

The new owners were very welcoming. They still had the same menu of drinks and very similar food items from which to choose.

Today, though, when I walked in, the place was empty. I asked how things were going. One of the new owners shared that things were starting to get better—that people were starting to come back.

Change can be hard for people. We like what we know. We are scared of what we don't know.

I was working with a client on her mindset and boundary setting, and she confessed, "I am so afraid that if I change, people won't like me."

We had to dig deeper. And she had to realize that people liked her pleasing them. They liked her being responsible for their happiness. But did they truly know her for who she authentically was? The truth was no. She was adapting to what other people wanted and what she perceived they needed her to be.

It is true that as you change and show up differently, people who are used to you one way will react. Some positive, and yes, some negative. Because again, change is hard. But people like me show up to the coffee shop even if there are new owners—others not so much.

But those who really love you will learn to love the way you show up, no matter what.

I think of it as "Love me, or love me."

I hear fear statements a lot actually. But what if we flip the script of fear? What if instead of accepting fear as simply "false emotion appearing real," we actually think of it simply as "face everything and rise up"?

If you knew that it was OK to be you, to be authentically you, how would you show up differently?

I'M SORRY

Every day brings a chance to live free of regret and with as much joy, fun, and laughter as you can stand.

OPRAH WINFREY

ONE DAY I was riding up the elevator. When it got to my floor, the doors opened. As I was exiting, I apologized to the people that were waiting to get on.

"I'm sorry," I said.

I got off the elevator and then kind of stopped in my tracks. I realized I had just apologized for exiting the elevator. What in the world?

Later that day I was talking to a friend and shared my experience and my reaction. She relayed a similar experience. A gentleman had startled her, and she apologized to him.

This got me thinking.

How often do we think we owe someone an apology for just being ourselves?

How often do we think we have to be sorry for setting boundaries that honor our personal values?

I know that with many of my clients, the fear of offending someone has kept them from setting boundaries. They don't want to cause conflict or be viewed as being rude.

But is it really your responsibility how someone else feels?

What if instead of thinking you are responsible for how

someone else feels, you realized all you could do is contribute to their feelings? If you are acting with good intentions, then do you owe anyone an apology?

This is the distinction of "responsible for" versus "contributing to."

If you were able to just set a few more boundaries in your life, and not be apologetic for them, what would be possible?

THE DMV

You alone are enough.
You have nothing to prove to anybody.
MAYA ANGELOU

I'VE SHARED ABOUT teaching child number two to drive. Well, he took his test a couple weeks ago . . . and passed—yay!

While we were at the DMV, we noticed that none of the workers were smiling. My son and I started to joke who would be the best option for his tester. He finally chose the gentleman at desk number 3.

A few minutes later, we heard the announcement: "Now serving A20 at desk 3." My son looked at me and smiled.

A few moments later, out walked my son along with Gentleman Number 3, scowl and all.

They were gone for about twenty minutes. And then in they walked.

I looked at my son and kind of waited for a response. He just shrugged. I had no idea what that meant. They walked back to desk number 3.

A few moments later my son waved me over to pay. Obviously, this meant that he had passed.

I walked over and sat down in the chair and began to fill out the necessary paperwork and execute payment. At one point, Gentleman Number 3 cracked a smile.

We thanked him, and my son and I walked out.

As we got to the car, my son turned to me and said, "How do you do that?"

What?" I said.

"I tried to get that man to smile the entire time. I didn't even know if I passed or failed because he hardly said a word. You walk over, and in seconds you got him to crack a smile. How do you do that with people?"

I smiled. And shrugged.

The truth is, I don't always make people smile. But I do show up.

I used to care if people were happy or sad. OK, the truth is that I do still care if they are happy or sad, but there is now a caveat to that. I used to think it was my responsibility. I now realize that it is not my responsibility how anyone feels; all I can do is contribute. So I just show up as me. I show up as genuinely as I can be. I am not happy all the time. I have my crap days and moments. But when I interact with people, I try my best to treat them with kindness and respect, and I honor their uniqueness as I have learned to honor mine. If that makes them smile, great. If not, I am OK with that too.

"I am just me," I said to my son, "and if that makes them happy, great. If not, that's their choice."

If you knew that you being you was more than enough, how would your relationships or interactions benefit?

SQUEEZED IN LIKE SARDINES

Our life is what our thoughts make it.
Marcus Aurelius

TRAVELING THIS PAST weekend, I ended up at an airport where you have to ride a bus from the terminal to the rental car area. Because all the rental car companies are housed in the same building, all the patrons of these companies and all their luggage ride one bus to retrieve their cars.

Here we were, all piled onto this bus. There was standing room only, and I could hardly move an inch without bumping into either another human or a suitcase of some kind.

It was really uncomfortable. But as we meandered from the airport to the rental car area, I started to think.

This is similar to what happens when our "inner back seat driver" likes to tell us everything we have done wrong or should have done differently. It just keeps going, filling our heads with negativity, with criticism. And all those thoughts just pile on in our minds.

The next thing we know, we can't think straight. We almost feel paralyzed to move forward. I know I certainly stop being able to have fluid thoughts. Instead it's just a feeling of stuckness, much the way I felt riding the bus at the airport.

How do we stop the "inner back seat driver"?

Maybe we don't try so hard. Honestly, it's going to happen.

The thoughts keep coming, much like the people that kept loading onto the bus. You cannot run from it. So sometimes you just need to slow down. Breathe. Observe. And then proceed.

Slowing down and observing the fact that the "inner back seat driver" is coming at you with lots of thoughts, you don't become attached to them. You don't judge them. Or try to fix them. Or even deal with them. You simply let them be there.

It's like riding the bus. With the crowd. Until they disperse.

Let the thoughts be. They will indeed crowd into your head. But as you become quiet, they will settle. They will quiet down.

If you gave yourself just 5 percent more space to be with your thoughts and leave that "inner back seat driver" alone rather than going into "fix it" mode, how would your world change?

A BOTTLENECK

*Everything is in motion. Everything flows.
Everything is vibrating.*
William Hazlitt

ONE EVENING I was cooking dinner. I started to pour olive oil into the pan from the little bottle we have near the stove. It was not pouring. I glanced over and realized I had turned the bottle too far upward. I needed to angle it so that some air could still get into the bottle, and therefore, the oil would actually have room to come out.

Later in the evening, my daughter was pouring the dog food from the new bag I had bought into the storage container we have. She called me over because the food was not coming out. I walked over and grabbed the bag alongside her. We moved it from an up-and-down position to a slightly tilted position. And the dog food started to flow.

It just needed to be angled. Again, allowing space allowed the food room to flow out into the container.

These instances really got me thinking.

These were bottlenecks.

That's what it's like in our heads sometimes. Our brains fill up with thoughts. With "ought tos," with "should." With a dialog from our inner critic. With expectations. The list goes on and on.

And the thoughts get stuck. They can't dissipate. They can't flow out. And then we feel stuck.

My heart has called me to work with people on learning to manage this type of "stuckness." My calling is to hold space. To meet people where they are. To offer time and judgment-free space. To support them as they find the ability to "tilt." To allow "some air" in so they can work through where they are stuck.

If you knew you were 100 percent supported as you made the "tilt" in your thinking, what would flow for you?

LESSONS FROM AN OLD DOG

*As you walk down the fairway of life you must smell the roses,
for you only get to play one round.*

BEN HOGAN

I AM A dog person.

I always have been. And my dogs mean the world to me. My Ridgeback is getting up there in age. He has had three bouts of cancer, which I think has caused him to age a bit more rapidly.

The thing about him is that he has always been my dog. He has always been in sync with me since his puppy days. On walks, he has always been ready to go. On a mission. Walking with a purpose. No sniffing, just walking. All business. (This goes great with a type A personality like me.)

Recently, though, on one of our walks, he started to do something he has never done.

He stopped to sniff the bushes and flowers along the walk.

As he did this, I stopped. Both physically and mentally.

I took notice.

He was pausing on his walk to sniff. To take in the experience. To enjoy it. It wasn't that he didn't have a purpose in his walk. He was just being present.

What if I took this lesson from him?

Instead of telling myself a story that I had to motor through my task list and that if I slowed down somehow, I was not working on purpose, what if I told myself I was simply being present? What would be possible?

If you gave you yourself 5 percent more grace each day to slow down in thought or action, what could you actually experience?

THE LOST KEYS

*We worry too much. We don't allow our bodies to heal,
and we don't allow our minds and hearts to heal.*
                    THICH NHAT HANH

THE OTHER DAY I heard this story.

A man was looking for his keys. He was searching high and low. He started to get frazzled and a little panicked. Then he saw a light outside.

He followed the light, thinking that maybe his keys were there. With the light, he thought they should be easier to spot.

His friend came along and asked what he was doing. He told his friend he was searching for his lost keys. The friend decided to help.

They searched and searched, until the friend finally asked, "When did you have the keys last?"

The man stopped.

He looked at his friend. He replied, "When I was in the house."

This story got me thinking.

What we seek for ourselves and about ourselves is not outside of us. Far too often we look outside of ourselves, thinking that's where answers lie or where we will "find ourselves." The truth is that we are already whole. And when and if we lose sight of that, we just need to look inside "our house." It's there. Ready to be found.

Are you ready to rediscover your authentic self? Because it's already there.

www.ingramcontent.com/pod-product-compliance
Lightning Source LLC
Chambersburg PA
CBHW030334100526
44592CB00010B/695